A Glance at Indian Economy
By
Chakrapani Srinivasa

A Glance at Indian Economy
By Chakrapani Srinivasa
Copyright 2018 Chakrapani Srinivasa

About the Author

Chakrapani Srinivasa (Padmaja), Freelance journalist from India possesses Bachelor degree in Engineering (B.E) and Post graduate in Business Management (MBA) with Distinction. He has worked as Associate Editor of 'Naradar' fortnightly journal in Chennai, India. He is the Senior Editor of the journal "The Divineness".

Contributed articles, short stories and travelogues in leading journals like Ananda Vikatan, Kumudam, Savi, Kalki, Dinamani Kadhir, Dinamani daily, Idhayam Pesukirathu, Naradar etc

He is the Consulting Editor: Contemporary Who's Who-Research Board of Advisers of ABI, USA.

Dedicated to my dear parents

Preface

This book deals with topics like Revenue in India, Methods to improve investment climate in India, Food statistics, short term measures for investment, Green India, Mal-nutritional Diseases in India, Nuclear storage in India, Food Security Bill, branches to be opened for foreigners etc. "A great book for reference" say the readers!!

Revenue in India

A stable government is essential for investment improvement in this nation, which is tormented by multi language, multi religion, caste and creed.

Controlling the deficit is the greatest challenge for the Delhi rulers. There are 3 types of deficits.

First is revenue deficit. Due to liberal reduction in tax, this deficit occurs in India. In 2011-12 it was 5% and in 2013 it came down to 3.5%.

Second deficit is budget deficit. In 2011-12 it rose to 5.3% of GDP.

Third deficit is primary deficit. It was 3.5% of GDP in 2011-12 and rose to 5.3% in 2013. Due to this sad condition, the industrial progress dropped down. It has been fixed as 3% in 2017-2018, say the government officials.

It is a practice to fix target for growth, but it is disappointing to fix target for downfall like financial deficit. Against the figure forecasted in 2011 – 12, the budget deficit increased by 40.9%. In 2011- 2012 it got worsened as it increased by 85.6%. Hence to manage this deficit, Reserve Bank print notes, but revenue is also not satisfactory. From April to November for the year 2010 -2011, we have obtained only 69.3% of the revenue target. Expenditure was 62.3%. In 2012 we obtained revenue only 48.2% of the anticipated figure and in 2013 it dropped down sadly to 46.5% of the expected revenue. But expenditure has risen by 60.5% in 2011 – 12 and by 58.2% in 2012 -13, against the target.

"How the revenue fell down so badly in India?" is the hot question asked by all tax payers. There are two ways to get revenue. One is from taxes and other is from other than taxes. Revenue from investment is the second category. In 2010 -11, the income referred as the first category was reduced to 47.6% from 69.9%. Income through investments came down from 60.8% in 2010 – 2011 to 21.14% in 2012 -2013. This income is obtained from sale of public sector shares.

The Delhi rulers do not aim to raise the revenue through tax levy, as it will hit the middle men and government employers, who are the major tax payers. Now the income from sale of shares held by government in PSU has become a tough task. Whenever any announcement is made, immediately the Communist party leaders join hands with union members and staff to agitate violently. Though the government aimed to get Rs.30000 crores for the sale of PSU shares, it failed to achieve it. To increase revenue, the Supreme Court showed a way in 2G case. As the license was cancelled a new license could have been issued to raise revenue. But unfortunately 2G spectrum shares were sold at lower value to cause loss to the government.

The Kelkar Committed has suggested selling the infrastructure held by Railways, Shipping and Forest division.

Communist leaders proclaim that India is a poor nation. Some leaders say that it is a middle class people nation. Economic experts say that India is a developing nation. But Congress may assure it to be a progressing nation. This progress is achieved only by FDI and sale of government owned property in India. This condition is pitiable.

When British rulers ruled India, we could get $1 for just Rs1. But now after 65 years, we have to pay Rs.65 to get a single dollar. So, independence has not improved our investment climate or economy.

By controlling import of gold, the rupee value may raise, felt the Finance Minister. Consequently, 4% tax was enforced for import of gold. In the next two days he raised it by 6%. Then it was raised to 8% and 10%. Even if it is raised by 100%, the craze for gold will not subsidize in this country, where a boy friend still calls his girl friend as 'my dear golden girl'. Due to intense pressure enforced by the Ministry of Finance, the price of gold has soared to Rs.30000 from Rs.19000.

So, the common man is the sufferer and his purse will be emptied. This will in turn destroy his purchasing power for other goods manufactured in India and kill the industrial growth. Eventually investment climate will fall back. Aiming to curb gold import is not a solution to build economy. Even if it is totally banned, it is not an essential item to live. Our main taboo for economy growth is crude oil. The import of it cannot be curbed. For all industrial production, transport and infrastructure developments we need crude oil. Already we are importing crude oil to the tune of $170 crore. Next is gold, which is imported to the value of $70 crore.

When a nation is struggling economically, it is not wise to invest such a huge amount for import of gold. Finance Minister has gone to the extreme level of advising citizens and women not to have craze for gold purchase. "These words can come from the mouth of a saint and not from a Finance Minister" say the women folks. Like copper, aluminum, iron etc, this is also a metal, says he, but the old lady at home replied of course "Gold is a metal. But a rupee is also mere paper".

"It has been planned to pledge 200 tons of gold in a multinational bank. For any emergency a middle class family man pledges gold in a pawn broker shop. A government also acts in a similar manner. When the government says gold is like copper, brass and iron, why it doesn't pledge these metals at multinational banks?" asks the man in the street

Actually the main asset for a nation is industrial production. This is represented by gold and currencies, say the experts. Gold has international value and an Indian woman wears it around her neck and ears, whereas a lady abroad stores it in her safe locker.

As the rupee value is undependable, people have faith for gold. As the nation prints currencies in a liberal manner, it may lead to a situation witnessed in Somalia. In this situation when gold reserve is poor, to solve the problem the Ministry for Finance will not allocate Rs.60 crores for import of gold, as a precautionary measure. But smuggling of gold will boost rapidly to meet the needs of the common man. If this inflation continues, then all will have money but no goods will be available in market. Barter trading will be witnessed in India.

Industrial production has come down to mere 1%. So, in this condition we have nothing to export. Only human beings in this poor

India have to be exported for procuring wheat, dhal and rice from developed countries. Car production has come down by 12% due to this fall in export. Foreign currency flow in India has come down drastically. Naturally the demand for dollar rose up and fall in Indian currency was the fatal result.

In 2003 to 2008 economy had a colorful period due to liberalization. But to control the investment, the government implemented stringent rules to avoid the Indian companies carrying heavy funds to foreign companies. This shattered the foreign investment in India as they feared that their investment will not fetch revenue.

In 1998, when Malaysia experienced financial crisis the government prevented the movement of funds to foreign countries. So, all the investments made in that country by MNCs was locked. This fear is now conquering India and MNCs will not come forward for further investments. This climate and financial trend should not take place. Government should erase that fear immediately to save our economy supported by developed nation.

Reserve Bank is planning to sell the dollars in its reserve to prevent the fall of rupee value. This is a short term measure only, say the experts.

If they lose dollars in hand then India will tumble down totally.

To improve investment climate technological up gradation is essential. Many obsolete methodologies still persists in Indian industries. This should be changed.

For the drop in industrial production we cannot blame the sluggishness of economic condition in 2008, because industrial production rose from 6.7% in 2008-09 to 8.6% in 2009-10 and 9.3% in 2010-11. When investment falls, usually production will fall. But here import of raw materials increased but production failed down.

In the past 5 years, import of raw materials affected the national production. When import enhanced, the local raw material suppliers were facing a collapse. When gross domestic production increased by 8.1%, the industrial progress was only 5.3%. Later raw material production faced a sliding by 4% in 2011-12 and 5.7% in 2012-13. For the past 3 years there is no progress in industrial production. Due to import of raw materials, the foreign goods entered like a Tsunami in Indian market. In 2001 -04, when BJP ruled, the import of foreign goods was only $600. In 2004 – 05 to 2012 import sharply raised by 8 times and $5.5 billion worth of goods were entering Indian market.

At this juncture GDP raised by 3.2%. Now after 9 years of rule the import has risen by $50 billion. Previous regime showed a figure of $2.3billion. So, import of raw materials destroyed Indian industrial growth. Manufactured goods were also imported to shatter the Indian industrial scenario.

This should be checked with vigilance.

****

Measures to Save Indian Economy

The contribution by Indian families to foreign exchange reserve is $335 billion. It is almost equivalent to current fiscal deficit amount. So, the government can aim and focus to draw more amounts from NRI to save the economy.

Trade deficit reduced the industrial production in India

Current account deficit reduced the domestic production by 0.8% in 2007-08, 1.5% in 2008 – 09, 2.1% in 2009 – 10, 1.4% in 2010 – 11, 2.6% in 2011 -12, 3.9% in 2012 – 13. If we eliminate this deficit, then domestic industrial production in India would have touched 10.8% in 2007 -08, 8.2% in 2008 -09, 10.7% in 2010 – 11, 8.8% in 2011 – 12, and 8.9% in 2012 – 13.

Gold and crude oil import swallowed the available foreign exchange. Out of total gold production, 25% to 33% is procured by Indians. Out of total petroleum products requirement only 25% is produced in India. Remaining 75% had to be imported, which causes financial crisis every year.

Now it is a disgrace that most of the imported petroleum products are also manufactured in India. Without any reason they are imported as the government permitted liberal inflow of foreign goods to India. This affected the total industrial production and revenue.

For the past 9 years, Rs.402 billion worth of gold, silver, diamond etc have been imported.

At the same time during 9 years $251 billion worth jewels have been exported from India. After reducing this value the deficit is only $151 Billion.

Similarly during the past 9 years we have imported petroleum products worth $804 billion. But export of Indian made petroleum products is to the tune of Rs279 billion. So, after deduction we have a deficit of $525, which is lower than $587.

For the past 5 years import of petroleum products is to the tune of $360 billion and at the same time we have imported raw materials to the value of $407 billion. "It is unavoidable to import petroleum products. But we could have cut short the raw materials. Why it was not done?" ask the economic experts. So, without any proper forecast the raw materials have been imported and caused current account deficit. This totally smashed the domestic production.

Due to fall in rupee value we have to spend $9500 crore more for import of crude oil. Situation has been created such that every year we will be spending $1.60 crore more in future.

Economic failure in India is not only due to fall in current fiscal deficit, but also due to liberal tax reductions and subsidiaries. For the past 10 years, custom duty has been brought down by 50% and due to this we were able to get imported goods at lower price.

In 2007 – 08 custom duty revenue was Rs.1 lakh crore. But in 2009 -10 it came down to Rs.0.83 lakh crore. At the same time import was done to the tune of Rs.8.4 lakh crore in 2007 -08 and it rose to Rs.13.74 lakh crore. Import was raised by 56%, but income reduced by 17% due to flooding of foreign raw materials and miserably the Indian domestic production fell flat. Tax reduction phenomenon escalated the fiscal deficit monstrously and rupee value came down disastrously.

India had to borrow due to increase of Rs.21.6 lakh crore in fiscal deficit after 2008. The current fiscal deficit continued after liberalization. This is a sad trend.

For the past 9 years India has obtained $205 FDI and we have invested $102 billion in foreign lands. After deduction we can see that we have been getting $103 billion of FDI. Foreign nationals have invested $124 billion in share market. After adding this value the foreign exchange is $227 billion. This is lower than the current fiscal deficit of $339 billion. It was unavoidable for India to get loan from outside world.

Short term loans obtained by India has enhanced from $4 billion to $170 billion, which is 17% escalation. Other major loans increased from $288 billion to $396 billion. Due to excess loans and FDI, expenditure raised from $4 billion to $16.5 billion. Current fiscal deficit of $339 billion swallowed the revenue of $227 billion due to investment and additional loan amount of $288 billion. The foreign exchange reserve rose from $180 billion to mere $292 billion. This is too low figure for a poor nation like India. Due to this financial crisis the foreign investors hesitated to invest in India.

In this critical condition Indian economy has been marginally saved by the bond issue by Commercial banks and Reserve Bank. It is a traditional practice of Indians to store their savings in banks. This helped the Indian economy. That's why extensive campaign to increase savings bank account holders is done by all banks now. In a year the amount saved by Indians in banks is to the tune of Rs.10 lakh crores. This saved the face of Indian economy.

"How current fiscal deficit was managed?" is the common question asked by all. This is done by the generous flow of funds from Indians employed in developed countries like USA, Germany, France, United Kingdom etc. Also amount transferred from accounts held abroad to Indian banks supported the financial crisis. The contribution by Indian families to foreign exchange reserve is $335 billion. It is almost equivalent to current fiscal deficit amount. So, the government can aim and focus to draw more amounts from NRI to save the economy.

This amount is obtained by the sentimental feelings of Indians to support their aged parents residing in India. If they fail to send that amount, then Indian government had to face the financial burden to support these aged citizens.

China is another taboo for Indian growth. In 2006 – 2007 import from China was 13%. But in 2011 -12 it raised to 17%. For the past 6 years, the fiscal deficit has increased by $175 billion due to China's interference in trade.

In 2001 -02 it was only $1 billion trade dealings with China. But now we face a mammoth figure of $325 billion. Raw materials to the worth of $150 billion have been imported from China. That country is not a dependable neighbor as it has trade links with Pakistan in the field of defense, railways, and Nuclear power etc. Any gain obtained by China will add more neighbor attacks from Pakistan and China. It is disturbing to know that China spends $63 billion for defense. So, the amount drawn from India to China in turn collapses safety of Indian borders. The economic growth of China is a disturbing factor for India geographically, as border areas are gradually conquered illegally by them. China attracts the Indian importers with low rates, as its foreign exchange reserve is strong. Hence many billion dollar worth of Chinese goods are entering every year to India, which affects Indian economy.

Immediate action is to be taken to curb this inflow.

****

Improvements for Investment Climate

The contribution by Indian families to foreign exchange reserve is $335 billion. It is almost equivalent to current fiscal deficit amount. So, the government can aim and focus to draw more amounts from NRI to save the economy.

Trade deficit reduced the industrial production in India

Current account deficit reduced the domestic production by 0.8% in 2007-08, 1.5% in 2008 – 09, 2.1% in 2009 – 10, 1.4% in 2010 – 11, 2.6% in 2011 -12, 3.9% in 2012 – 13. If we eliminate this deficit, then domestic industrial production in India would have touched 10.8% in 2007 -08, 8.2% in 2008 -09, 10.7% in 2010 – 11, 8.8% in 2011 – 12, and 8.9% in 2012 – 13.

Gold and crude oil import swallowed the available foreign exchange. Out of total gold production, 25% to 33% is procured by Indians. Out of total petroleum products requirement only 25% is produced in India. Remaining 75% had to be imported, which causes financial crisis every year.

Now it is a disgrace that most of the imported petroleum products are also manufactured in India. Without any reason they are imported as the government permitted liberal inflow of foreign goods to India. This affected the total industrial production and revenue.

For the past 9 years, Rs.402 billion worth of gold, silver, diamond etc have been imported.

At the same time during 9 years $251 billion worth jewels have been exported from India. After reducing this value the deficit is only $151 billion.

Similarly during the past 9 years we have imported crude oil worth $804 billion. But export of Indian made petroleum products is to the tune of Rs279 billion. So, after deduction we have a deficit of $525, which is lower than $587.

For the past 5 years import of Petroleum products is to the tune of $360 billion and at the same time we have imported raw materials to the value of $407 billion. It is unavoidable to import petroleum products. But we could have cut short the raw materials. "Why it was not done?" ask the economic experts. So, without any proper forecast raw materials have been imported and caused current account deficit. This totally smashed the domestic production.

Due to fall in rupee value we have to spend $9500 crore more for import of crude oil. Situation has been created such that every year we will be spending $1.60 crore more in future.

Economic failure in India is not only due to fall in current fiscal deficit, but also due to liberal tax reductions and subsidiaries. For the past 10 years, custom duty has been brought down by 50% and due to this we were able to get imported goods at lower price.

In 2007 – 08 custom duty revenue was Rs.1 lakh crore. But in 2009 -10 it came down to Rs.0.83 lakh crore. At the same time import was done to the tune of Rs.8.4 lakh crore in 2007 -08 and it rose to Rs.13.74 lakh crore. Import was raised by 56%, but income reduced by 17% due to flooding of foreign raw materials and Indian domestic production fell flat. Tax reduction phenomenon escalated the fiscal deficit monstrously and rupee value came down disastrously.

India had to borrow due to increase of Rs.21.6 lakh crore in fiscal deficit after 2008. The current fiscal deficit continued after liberalization. This is a sad trend.

For the past 9 years India has obtained $205 FDI and we have invested $102 billion in foreign lands. After deduction we can see that we have been getting $103 billion of FDI. Foreign nationals have invested $124 billion in share market. After adding this value the foreign exchange is $227 billion. This is lower than the current fiscal deficit of $339 billion. It was unavoidable for India to get loan from outside world.

Short term loans obtained by India has enhanced from $4 billion to $170 billion, which is 17% escalation. Other major loans increased from $288 billion to $396 billion. Due to excess loans and FDI, expenditure raised from $4 billion to $16.5 billion. Current fiscal deficit of $339 billion swallowed the revenue of $227 billion due to investment and additional loan amount of $288 billion. The foreign exchange reserve rose from $180 billion to mere $292 billion. This is too low figure for a poor nation like India. Due to this financial crisis the foreign investors hesitated to invest in India.

In this critical condition Indian economy has been marginally saved by the bond issue by Commercial banks and Reserve Bank. It is a traditional practice of Indians to store their savings in banks. This helped the Indian economy. That's why extensive campaign to increase savings bank account holders is done by all banks now. In a year the amount saved by Indians in banks is to the tune of Rs.10 lakh crores. This saved the face of Indian economy.

"How current fiscal deficit was managed?" is the common question asked by all. This is done by the generous flow of funds from Indians employed in developed countries like USA, Germany, France, United Kingdom etc. Also amount transferred from accounts held abroad to Indian banks supported the financial crisis. The contribution by Indian families to foreign exchange reserve is $335 billion. It is almost equivalent to current fiscal deficit amount. So, the government can aim and focus to draw more amounts from NRI to save the economy.

This amount is obtained by the sentimental feelings of Indians to support their aged parents residing in India. If they fail to send that amount, then Indian government had to face the financial burden to support these aged citizens.

China is another taboo for Indian growth. In 2006 – 2007 import from China was 13%. But in 2011-12 it raised to 17%. For the past 6 years the fiscal deficit has increased by $175 billion due to China's interference in trade.

In 2001-02 it was only $1 billion trade dealings with China. But now we face a mammoth figure of $325 billion. Raw materials to the worth of $150 billion have been imported from China. That country is not a dependable neighbor as it has trade links in defense, railways, and Nuclear power etc with Pakistan. Any gain obtained by China will add more neighbor attacks from Pakistan and China. It is disturbing to know that China spends $63 billion for defense. So, the amount drawn from India to China in turn collapses safety of Indian borders. The economic growth of China is a disturbing factor for India geographically, as border areas are gradually conquered illegally by them. China attracts the Indian importers with low rates as its foreign exchange reserve is strong. Hence many billion dollar worth of Chinese goods are entering every year to India, which affects Indian economy.

Hence immediate action is to be taken to curb this inflow.

****

Branches Further To Be Opened For Foreigners

Introduction of US based defense equipments are a must for India. Their entry will add confidence and moral courage for our army men.

Banking is an important sector to be opened for foreigners to make a sea change in India. Right from customer service inside the bank premises to ATM at various locations, the quality of service is unsatisfactory. The improper handling of layman's saving account, facilities given to boost confidence of these poor class investments and infrastructure arrangements are black marks in all banks in India.

The safety in ATMs is a big head ache for the bank management. They openly state that they have insufficient funds to provide security guards in their ATMs, which leads to looting and murders. Also it is a pity that most of the time the ATMs will be out of service. Travelers depending on it are in desperate mood due to non-availability of cash and server problems. The banks spend a lot to advertise to use ATM debit cards but fail to maintain their ATMs. There is a big labor problem and lack of technical know-how in ATM operation, which leads to the government to handover bank operations to foreign experts. Liberalization in this sector will lead to better employment opportunities and lucrative salary pack.

Another field to be liberalized is Airways. The present airport facilities are in sufficient and below in quality. Falling of roof top in Chennai Meenambakkam air-port is one fine example of insipid maintenance practices followed there. The toilets emanate foul smell and water supply failure is a common feature. Abominable manner in which the air passengers are treated can be solved only by liberalization.

Next is the Railway division. The stoppage of trains due to stinking toilets, Battalion of bugs in A/c coach, age-old railway track safety gadgets and practices etc have agitated the tax payers. The contaminated catering service has lead to vomiting and attack of virus diseases to passengers. Hence quality is an urgent need for all train services. Using a single track system in many railway routes causes delays due to rail crossing phenomenon.

To see passengers squatting above the railway coaches during festival days is an eyesore. Improper planning of trains to meet the heavy crowd during that time has to be set right. Around 50 passengers travelling above compartments were jammed to death when a train crossed a tunnel in North India. So, train management can be liberalized to enable hassle free travelling to Indian voters.

Many illiterates are not capable of handling their income to survive during retired life. So, a reasonable and well managed agency is needed to handle their savings and then hand it over to them at the time of retirement in a proper fashion. The amounts collected from them have to be securely saved and also enhanced.

Pension fund is now handled by about 7 agencies, among which some are privately owned companies. It was opposed initially by the people and demanded the government to give pension. They also demanded that pension fund should be handled by government organization only. But private companies were permitted. Now the people oppose the FDI in this sector. Their protests are absurd.

Pension is similar to insurance fund. Both will be under the same rules and regulations, but the controlling authorities will be different. LIC offered insurance and later private organizations were allowed to do that. So, this gave room for many investors to select. FDI in this sector has to be enhanced to get better service with safety and quality.

When government is unable to disburse the pension fund, then the people have to handle it with proper saving measures. But they do not have the capacity to do that. So the amount saved for them had to handle dexterously and built up fruitfully. The only solution for it is more FDI in this sector.

Defense is another important sector, where furthered liberalization is needed. The present technology is not adequate to face the growing terrorism in India. Modernized guns, ammunitions and submarines are needed. Introduction of US based defense equipments are a must for India. Their entry will add confidence and moral courage for our Indian army men. Appropriate training is readily offered with goodwill and broadmindedness by US defense experts. Imported UAV, radars, helicopters etc will add strength to India to manage border issues.

Healthcare is another sector, which needs uplift. Present attention in Indian hospitals is weak and inadequate malnutrition kills newborn babies in all States. Maternity care is poor and ratio between population and number of beds is also not encouraging. The entry of foreign nationals is needed now to solve the health crisis.

****

Green India

Change the Trend

Nowadays the green fields are converted as concrete flats, residential complexes and industries. Also the younger generations spend more time on computers and their extracurricular activities are nil. In this situation the youths have no chance to learn about agriculture, which is the back bone of India.

To change this trend and to make all children to learn about agriculture and green India movement, the students in Sri Vivekananda Vidyavanam in Thiruparaithurai are taught about cultivation. Its Headmaster Masimalai has induced all students to undergo training in the adjacent 5 acres lands belonging to Thapovanam. Basic activities involved in agriculture like land preparation, plugging, sowing etc are practically demonstrated with the help of farmers. Students take keen interest in irrigation, planting of saplings to grow vegetables, rice and dhal.

The products obtained are utilized in their hostel mess and also sold to teachers at low rates. The amount earned out of it is used to meet the school expenses also. They grow 10 to 15 kilos of Ladies fingers once in four days. Wherever water is seen in abundance, they grow herbal plants to serve the medicinal field. Hundreds of herbs are now seen, which rejoices the Ayurveda doctors. Whenever a teacher does not turn up, the students are sent to field to grow paddy and vegetables.

The students in their hostel use the herbal leaves they grow for any cough, cold fever and body pain. They do not approach any doctor for medical treatment.

These students will make India green in future, as most of them have decided to spend their lifetime in cultivation only.

No Diesel

Battery operated equipment in the field is rare. Most of the farmers use diesel operated farming equipments, which spoil the atmosphere.

So, Raghunath, a diploma holder in Electrical and Electronics has created equipment with gearbox, 12v motor and cutting nail. We can operate it for 3hrs and without interruption it is easily chargeable and transported to any location. The student hails from Pudupakkam in Pondicherry State.

Labor Problem

The Green India movement is affected mainly due to non-availability of manpower. Nobody is willing to take up this profession and they seek I.T. jobs in town. So, whenever cultivation is done, all the green fields are destroyed and neglected for want of men and women. To solve this issue the villagers in Muthupattinam, Sethidal and Senkudil in Thiruvadanai Taluk, Ramnad district adopt a new way.

All the farmers have formed groups and if land owners request for men and women they arrange for it at a reasonable daily wage. Previously in all villagers all farms had permanent employees. But later on these laborers acquired lands and hence there was shortage of men to work in fields. The lands owners cultivated with the help of relatives, which did not work out well.

So, they demanded agricultural laborers for their fields. This eventually raised the daily wage of the laborers. To solve this, a group was formed like Women Self Help Group and supplied men and women to work in fields. This lowered the tension of land owners for cultivation works undertaken in Ramnad district. In each group there are 20 to 40 laborers. Even for the work force requirements in nearby villages, these men and women are sent by tractors and tempos. Anybody can be made to work in any Taluk or village. Previously this system was not in existence and the sons of the soil were alone permitted to do cultivation in that particular village. But this group system enabled the green India movement to grow and flourish in all villages. This system is in existence for the past 2 years.

Previously the daily wage was Rs.30 to Rs.40/day. Now it is Rs.150 to Rs.180/day. The group had only 20members initially and now it has increased to 50. Their relatives alone assisted for cultivation works. Later on all nearby village land owners requested this group to send manpower for harvest etc. The group in Muthupattinam in Ramnad is the most busy and popular team. Another great advantage is that they offer same salary pack to both men and women. This attracted many women to join the Green India movement in this district.

Previously women will earn only 50% less than men. This made women to evade cultivation works. But now the trend has changed. They have requests from Zamindars in Sivaganga, Pudukottai etc and incentives are given to boost their interest. There is no broker or third party interference in wage payment. Immediate availability of man power is another advantage.

In yester years the land owners has to step into each hut and request the family head to send their sons and daughters for cultivation works. Many will refuse and this delayed the harvest works and cause loss. Now that problem is solved as the agriculture groups immediately arrange for workers to do the cultivation in time.

Children to Cultivate

Madurai has set an example for youths through Resource Centre for Participatory Development studies. This center aims for Green India and Clean India and improved agricultural status. It will be surprised to know all the participants of this NGO are children. Group discussions, planning and execution are done by children only. Experts in RCPDS guide them and act as mentors.

The changing global temperature, ozone, methods of using patricides, nature cultivation and disadvantages of improper food storage are taught to them. Child Panchayat is associated with this NGO. During school holidays they are all involved in agriculture to make India green. The local Panchayat authorities have allocated 10 acres of land for these children to cultivate rice, dhal and vegetables. The children plough, sow seeds and irrigate with their own hands. They use only natural manure obtained from cow dung. Nature specialists like Nammalwar visit and encourage green fields in that area.

Most of the schools in India teach Physics, Chemistry, and Maths to enter engineering colleges to become I.T engineers. To break this trend the children in that district are taught about agriculture to see that each child when he or she grows owns a few acres of lands to grow trees, plants and essential grains for India to survive.

Heaps of Herbs

Salem district is proud of Palanivelu, who organized MGP to produce Coleus herbs from 4000 acres of land and earn a turnover of Rs.80crore.

Palanivelu hails from Manjini village Anthur Taluk, Salem District. When all youths were mad after computers, he wished to study about agriculture. Many laughed and giggled. Even though he secured a government job after his Bsc in Agriculture, he left that job and showed interest to grow Coleus herbs.

When entire world seeks medicines, which have no side effects, his interest to grow herbal plants to produce valuable medicines was intensified. There is a great demand for herbs like Avuri, Nithyakalyani, Kanvallikizhangu and Senganthazh malar and was sent abroad in large quantities to earn millions. They were cultivated on contract basis. So, he started cultivation of Coleus, a type of herbal plant like Karpooravalli, suitable to cure coughs, sore throat, and cold and lung problems.

In Salem district he grew this Coleus in a small scale and later on it grew widely as there was great demand from foreign buyers. Seeing the growth of these rare herbs, many leading MNCs agreed to buy it and requested him to grow it on 1000 acres. He was the only person to grow herbs as agreement basis in India. His MGP became popular and now they are cultivating Coleus on 4000acres of land and also he has planned to grow it in 20 districts. The agriculturalists are abundantly happy to see that income, which has crossed Rs.80crores turnover.

Even a software company could not have achieved this Himalayan heights, but the aspirations of an individual to make India green has touched that land mark.

He has proved that Green India is in the hands of future generation!

****

Mal-nutritional Diseases in India

Setbacks

Ignorance, illiteracy, poverty and economic backwardness are the root causes of malnutrition diseases in India.

Population growth is unbearable. Millions are added every year in spite of multifarious family welfare propaganda and programs.

Urban slum areas, populations in draught situations and acid rain regions, poor industrial workers, citizens affected by natural calamities and tribal populations are the most affected sectors regarding malnutrition.

India is unable to face the setbacks in spite of many aids from various countries.

Apart from nutritional food items recent survey revealed that 30% of Indian population are unable to buy what they basically want for survival.

Punjab, Haryana and M.P 4.5 oz of pulses and satisfactory quantity of milk are consumed per day when compared to Kerala, Tamil Nadu where only 10g of pulses is consumed. Also it is saddening to see that 15% of population had adequate calories precipitin, while 10% the daily calories intake was even less than 1500 Kcal. Protein intake of about 60gm/day loan found in 50% but animal protein constituted only less than 10%. It is also disturbing to note that 27% of household in India were protein deficient and 10% were calories deficient.

In a research study by health authorities it was found that majority of women in reproductive phase were underweight, their weights ranging from 35 to 40kg. 40% were suffering from Vitamin B complex deficiency, 15% from hypovitaminosis A, 10% from hypo proteinemia and 56% had hemoglobin value than 10gm percent.

Some customer and traditional practices based on superstition have adversely affected the nutritional intake of many millions.

Various nutritional deficiencies like polyneuritis, angular stormatitis, glossitis and anemia are the netresults.

ISI allowance is 30,000 bacterial per ml of pasteurized milk. But 2.4 million per ml was found in pasteurized milk in Mumbai. So, new technology has also killed the nutrition intake of men, women and children in India. At times mice and cockroaches have been found in milk bottles in Delhi and consumer protection members have raised their voice against it. Worms in chocolates of some popular brand was noticed in Mumbai.

So, various reasons cause malnutrition and ill health in India.

In India some popular nutritional diseases absented in various parts of the country is listed below.

1) Protein – calorie malnutrition
2) Vitamin deficiency
3) Thiamine deficiency
4) Pellagra
5) Ariboflavinosis
6) Hypovitaminosis C: Survey
7) Hypovitaminosis D-Rickets and osteomalacia
8) Nutritional anemias
9) Lathyrism
10) Aflatoxicosis
11) Epedemic dropsy
12) Endemic goiter
13) Endemic fluorosis
14) Veno-occlusive disease

Incidence of Kwashiorkor among the downtrodden is found to be 2-3%. For every case of Kwashiorkor there was observed as many as two of marasmus in India and also as many as a hundred of nutritional dwarfing. It was also found by Nutritional Society of Hyderabad that incidence of Kwarhiorkor was estimated at 2-3% and PCM observed in

15% of all children. Growth retardation was found to range from 80% to 100%.

National Institute of Nutrition ICMR Hyderabad has revealed that there exists mild attack of PCM in Punjab, Haryana and Eastern States; moderate attacks in Jammu & Kashmir, Gujarat, U.P, M.P, Rajasthan, Bihar, Assam and Northern parts of Maharashtra and severe attack of PCM in West Bengal, Orissa, Andhra Pradesh, Mysore, Kerala, Tamil Nadu and Southern parts of Maharashtra. The regional office of South East Asia of WHO has revealed that non-availability of enough or good food for infant children, faulty feeding habits, prejudices, superstitions, supplementary food mainly cereal based given only late in infancy, poor environmental hygienic conditions found in places like Dharavi in Mumbai, slums of West Bengal & Orissa.

In India it is reported that 1 million have become blind in early childhood due to deficiency in Vitamin A. Every year 15000 children become blind in India.

The Vitamin A deficiency is found abundantly in Eastern and Southern parts of India. A study was conducted in Mumbai and it was observed that 13% of population were affected by Conjunctiva Xerosis says the Nutrition Society of India. Also it is pathetic to note that 58-66% of preschool and school children from rural poor class and 33-48% of urban poor class pregnant or workmen were affected. Main reason the affected child is not brought to the notice of a doctor but taken to a local health worker.

For want of funds, facilities and basic infrastructure the downtrodden is unable to go for better consultation or treatment. The age group most affected in India is between 1-5years and as many as 5-10% of the toddles have been reported to be suffering from clinical deficiency and hence 14% of children are blind.

Males are affected more than females in India with a ratio of 3:2.

Conjuctive Xerosis has not been found common during pregnancy. Night Blindness has been reported for many young kids.

The attack of Xerosis in children was more between 3-5 years, minimum in 18 months and rapidly decline after 5years.

In school children above 6 years 67% were found to have mild changes and very few had signs of advanced deficiency. A survey was conducted in Tamil Nadu and it was found that Bitot's spots were found to be 5% and it was more common in older children as compared to younger ones.

It is observed that deficit of Vitamin A is maximum in the Eastern and Southern States of India. The worst sufferers are infants as their daily intake was seen to be 100-150I4 of vitamin A and 230-300I4 of beta carotene as compacted with recommended daily allowances.

Thiamine deficiency (Beriberi) was endemic in practically whole of coastal region of Andhra Pradesh from Chennai to Vishakapattinam. Calorie intake in different States is also a cause for mal-nutritional diseases in India.

The average daily calorie and protein intake per head is high in Madhyapradesh (3000kcal) amongst all States in India. The least is in Tamil Nadu.

In most rural areas of U.P, M.P and Orissa it was found that mothers from poor socio economic groups received an average daily of only 1875 calories, proteins 44gm, calcium 375mg calories, proteins 44gm, calcium 375mg and iron 18mg says a medical report.

In future, Marasmus has chances of becoming even more common in India than what is not due to drop in breast feeding, poor socio economic background and poor environment.

Indian has half of world's 15 million blind persons and it is increasing day by day. Milder forms of thiamine deficiency presenting as calf tenderness, absence of knee and ankle jerks and general weakness and lowered physical capacity have been reported in many parts of India. The other vulnerable groups are Indian pregnant or lactating women and persons engaged in hard physical or mental activity in industrial areas of Mumbai, Kolkata, Orissa and Punjab.

Beriberi is predominant among rice eaters in India. In Northern states wheat is the main diet but not in Southern States.

Pellagra caused by niacin or nicotine acid deficiency is most common in the Deccan Plantain and some parts of Rajasthan. Nearly 1.1% admitted in general hospitals and 8-10% admitted in mental hospitals belongs to this category in India.

Pellagra in intimately related with poor sanitation, poverty and consumption of monotonous low quality diet (some deficient in niacin).

Ariboflavinosis - The primary reason for this disease in India is due to overall deficiency of riboflavin in average Indian diet in spite of widespread distribution of this Vitamin in common foods. The recommended allowance is 0.55mg per 1000kcal. But the average intake in India is only 0.30mg per 1000kcal. This is because we mainly depend upon cereals and pulsar for this Vitamin (for 79% of total requirement against 7% or 70 from milk).

In a medical survey in Tamil Nadu, Angular Stormatitis was found in 41% of children. In Mumbai 6% of pre-school children showed one or more signs viz angular stormatitis, cheilosis, red and raw tongue with atrophic or hypotrophy papillae. Angular stormatitis was the commonest sign (3.3%) being in many cases associated with protein calorie malnutrition. Deficiency signs of Ariboflavinosis are almost constantly present in cases of pellagra also.

In another survey conducted in Mumbai 4% of all preschool children had some signs of rickets and the overall incidence of clinically detectable epiphysis enlargement was 3.5% and radio logical abnormality 5%.

Nutritional anemia is prevalent in most of the Indian pregnant women. A study was conducted on 500 normal pregnant women in Chennai and it showed hemoglobin values between 10.5gm% to 11.5gm in only 10. None had values more than 11.5gm% It is also to be noted that 70%

had values between 8.7gm% and 10.15 gm%. This is as per Nutrition Society of India.

In Delhi 43% of pregnant women in Urban areas were found anemic and in rural areas 47% were found anemic. The transferring saturation was less than 15% in both groups. Further 18% of rural non pregnant females had hemoglobin 12gm% or more and almost half of them had transferring saturation less than 15% in both the groups. Also only 18% of rural non-pregnant females had hemoglobin 12gm% or more and almost half of them had transferring saturation less than 15%.

The overall figures on the basis of surveys conducted in Kolkata, Hyderabad, Trivandrum and Vellore were that 30-70% of pregnant females had hemoglobin less than 10gm%. In cities like Lucknow, Hyderabad and Chennai 21% of non-pregnant females had hemoglobin 10gm% or less and 42% of pregnant females had similar values. In another study in the hilly regions of the northern east it was found that 63.4% of all pregnant women had hemoglobin less than 10gm% and B-16 of all population had hemoglobin below 8gm%.

In Andaman & Nicobar Islands 51-8-77% are anemia. Males are lesser in number than females, say the medical reports. In villages of Himalayas at 12000 heights, the hemoglobin values were lesser than the desired values.

Amongst the number of sufferers in Tamil Nadu 40% of children had low value (less than 10-15gm %).

In India it is wearying to note that 54% of children suffer from anemia and the average preschool child reached the maximum hemoglobin level of only 11gm%. In another survey by medical authorities it was found that in India 79% of children aged between 6 to 36months admitted in AIIMS, New Delhi had low hemoglobin level. (<10gm %) and 90% had iron deficiency.

In many hilly regions in Indian a study was conducted on anemia and it was found that 35-83% of children had low hemoglobin level (less than 10gm %). Thus the overall figure for our country 50% of preschool children had low level of hemoglobin maternal mortality per 100,000 live births in India is 252 to 372 as per the survey of Nutrition Atlas of India.

Anemia is the commonest complication of pregnancy. A study revealed that 20% of maternal death was due to anemia in Chennai.

Anemia is mainly caused in India due to poor intake of food containing iron.

6% of average class in India had dietary iron less than 15mg per head per lay and 10% less than 20mg.

According to medical survey in India it is fond that average iron intake is only 5.9mg per day as compared to the recommended 1520mg. In Andaman the average daily intake is only 60.80%.

In our diet majority of the iron provided by aerials and pulses which supply 1.5mg and 2.8mg respectively. They form about 50% of the total dietary iron and that is where the problems shoot up in Indian families because of the presence of high amounts of phytates, which have been conclusively shown to destroy the iron absorption.

The Indian nutrition specialists have stated that much less iron is available to body from Indian food stuffs than believed. It was found that whereas in the rice based diets up to 5.5% of iron was assimilated. In the wheat based diets the correspondent figures were 1.5 – 2.1% and in the millet based only 1.6-1.7% as compared to 20% in the western diets.

Hookworms and Trichuris, the tiny helminths are common in rural areas of India. Though they suck only a small amount of blood per day very severe type of anemia will shoot up if it continues for a longer period.

These worms are fairly common in India and it lays 5000 eggs and makes an iron loss between 2 to 8mgpercent in an Indian body. It was found in Kolkata that 78 out of 180 were found iron deficient.

Malaria is also a popular disease in India as sanitation, drainage; open wells and polluted stagnant waters are found in plenty in various States. Recently more and more of Falciparum malaria are coming to the notice of health authorities. It is found prominent in Eastern, Northern and Southern States. In Andaman Nicobar Islands it was found 41% of the cases admitted in the hospitals are malaria affected patients.

A study in India revealed that 59 out of 180 cases of iron deficiency anemia with uterine bleeding, functional or due to fibroids, polyps or cancer, ceramic peptic ulcers, esophageal varices, hemorrhoids, dysenteries and blood from gums.

Amongst the anemic patients 33 had problems in Uterus, 13 in hemorrhoids and 12 in duodenum and one had problem in nose.

Also blood loss was also caused by excessive heat and humidity in India. Daily losses have been estimated to vary from 0.58 to 3.22mg with an average of 1.7mg in places like Rajasthan.

Nutrition to pregnant ladies in India is neglected and too many suffer due to anemia. Illiteracy and economic backwardness cause the damages to their life.

In a medical research study in Kolkata 20% of the patients had B12 deficiency, 50% had folic acid deficiency and 30% had both deficiencies.

Almost all in the B12 deficiency group were vegetarians. The frequency of megalo blastic anemia in south India has been estimated to be as high as 50% of all the pregnant and lactating female. In another study 39% of the children were found to be anemic and had megalo blastic marrow and major folic acid deficiency.

A study was conducted in Delhi for children in the age group of 3 months to 12 years. About 49% were B12 deficient, 90% were deficient in iron and 5% were total deficient.

Nutritional Research Laboratory of India conducted a study from which they found that 60% of patients with tropical spur were found to be having megaloblastic marrow associated with or without anemia and had defective absorption of Vitamin B12 and folic acid.

Further 15% had only Vitamin B12 deficiency, 30% had pure folic acid deficiently and 55% a combined folic acid and B12 deficiency.

Lathyrism is a crippling disease not widespread to every part of India but affected farming members of our society. Around 32,000 victims were reported affected in Rura and Satna in Madhya Pradesh alone. In some survey the incidence was found to be nearly 4% of the population, predominantly males.

A study of 200 families was done and the occurrence of lameness was detected to be 3 per 100 persons; all were youth and one time bread winners.

Epidemiology is found in agriculturally backward areas in the region of Sindhya Mountains with low yearly rain fall and poor irrigational facilities. This disease is caused by eating the pulse given instead of wage for the hard work they do as slaves to their masters, the land lords. They are high protein content obtained from Lathyrus plant which grows easily without manure or irrigation. It has been found that harmful effects could be seen by diet in 2-4 months time if it continued more than 40% of the pulse.

The affected families were found to be consuming 4 times the amount of pulse as compared to non-affected ones. Further it is seen that patients of Lathyrism in general consumed two thirds or more of their food as the pulse.

Therefore, those who eat in smaller amounts and mix it with other cereals or pulses, escape even if they continue to eat it for a pretty long time. Sometime back when famine occurred in Maharashtra, the people had no other go but to eat this Lathyrus pulse. The Indian Council for Medical Research has shown a way to remove the fix in it i.e. by boiling it and throwing away the water, which removes 90% of the toxin.

Aflatoxicosis is a disease caused by consuming toxin contained in a fungus called Aspergillums flatus. These grow not only in the seeds of groundnut but also of sun flower maize and soya bean. Much of the toxin is retained in the oil cake after expelling of the oil from the seeds. It was noticed when a consignment of groundnut cake for consumption of farm animals caused liver necrosis, jaundice and a large number of deaths, which happened in U.K.

Epedemic of acute aflatoxicity was noticed in Western India. It occurred in tribal villages of Gujarat and Rajasthan. The males were affected more than females. Clinically the features were jaundice, rapidly developing ascetic, portal hypertension and massive gastro intestinal bleeding. The mortality rate was high, out of 272 affected in the Panchmahal district of Gujarat 76 died in acute phase.

The source of the outbreak was due to the fact that maize was heavily contaminated with Aspergillums flatus. The toxity content of the contaminated food was as high as 6.25 to 15.6 ppm. It means that the affected person has consumed as much as 2-6mg of the toxin daily for almost for one month. When nuts and seeds are soiled with poor storage and are under poor storage these funguses grow quickly. The food grains when get soiled in flood calamities in Andhra Pradesh, were found to have such fungus.

Epidemic dropsy is a well known nutritional disorder restricted to India. Most of the time it is misdiagnosed as allergic edema, nephritic syndrome, beriberi, starvation, dermatitis, rheumatic heart disease, congestive heart failure, gastroenteritis, insect bites etc. The classical and constant symptom is swelling over feet coming after walking and increasing towards the evenings.

This epidemic outbreak was first noticed in Kolkata. It killed many laborers there. Then occurrences were seen in Nagpur, Hyderabad, New Delhi, Varanasi, Patna and Lucknow. Almost 200 were affected in Nagpur and 475 were affected in Kolkata. In Andhra Pradesh at Sirpur Kaghazanagar 230 individuals were affected. Usually groups of families are affected. Middleclass families are worst affected. The overall mortality is about 5% and in some epidemics it was high as 50%.

Endemic Goiter, an unsightly attack due to iodine is affecting the masses in different parts of India. Govt of India has totally banned non-iodized salt because of this.

The regions affected are sub-Himalayan regions and parts of adjoining plains. The highest rates were in girls between 12-18 years and boys between 9-13 years of age. The total number of cases estimated was 40 million based on recent survey.

Areas affected are Northern U.P districts of Philibhit, Bareilly, Bacharach, Gonda, Basti, Gorakhpur, Northern Bihar in Muzafarpur, Champran, Darjeeling, Sikkim, Bhutan, parts of

Assam, Golpara, Lushai, Naga Hills and places like Tripura, Aijal, Imphal and Sibasagar, Dinajpur and Rangapur (Bangladesh). Other affected areas are Aravalli range and neighborhood of Luni river tributaries in Ajmer extending south of the Luni and Aravalli for about 300 miles, then to the Narmada River. In M.P, Jhansi, Lalitpur near Jabalpur, Sambalpur, Ranchi etc are affected areas.

In the south are along Western Ghats, Mahableshwar and Sahyadri and Bijapur Coimbatore and then Nilgiris Hills. Pune, banks of Cheyyar are also note worthy of these attacks.

Total affected persons rose from around 5 million to 40 million, says medical report. The attack was seen at 11.71% in Muzaffarpur district of Bihar and in some villages it was high as 50% to 70%. The school children in Ambala were affected up to 70%. Pathankot, Kangra and Gurdaspur showed rates of 30 to 90%. In Sikkim rate of attack was 61.5%. In Himalayan foot hills this disease covered 40% of the population.

Endemic fluorosis caused by intake of excess fluoride, which affects the teeth in children and skeletal system of adults.

This was reported in Chennai, Andhra Pradesh, Punjab, Karnataka, UP etc. Many cases were reported from Nalgonda, Prakasam and Guntur district. In Punjab State Bhatinda is one amongst the severely attacked. About 358 villages in Bhatinda were reported to be affected by this disease. It was found in 67% of children between 5-17 years. In some villages 30% of the entire population reported to be affected in this area. Out of these 19.7% had latent condition, 58.6% were without crippling defects, 13.3% were with crippling deformities and 8.4 % were advanced cases with neurological complications.

Fluorosis is found only in those areas where the fluoride content of drinking water is high. In a study in Punjab the incidence of fluorosis was found to be roughly proportional to the fluoride content of drinking water. Villages with 1.4 ppm of fluoride in drinking water had fewer than 10% of the cases, while those with 2.3 ppm had 30% cases. It was found that fluoride occurs only in areas with drinking water fluoride above 1-2 ppm.

Recently in Punjab reports of cancer were found and there was a big hue and cry due to it.

Veno occlusive disease in liver is an acute sub acute or chronic state of poisoning caused by consumption of Alkaloids of Crotalaria, Heliotropism or Seneca plants.

There was an outbreak of this disease in Madhyapradesh a long time back causing hundreds of deaths. The first two villages, to be affected were Navadi and Sabad. There was a report of 112 deaths and 219 cases in Bihar State.

****

Nuclear Storage in India

No modification or re-allocation can be done in labs, where radioactive materials are used. Radiation Safety Cell will give approval in writing for any changes in storage.

Challenging Issue

The nuclear storage is a challenging issue for any country.

Radiation Safety Committee is the authorized team to take care of storage and steps to avert any hazards.

Director and Radiation Safety Officer join hands with Radiation Safety Committee for all nuclear storage activities. They monitor that exposure is safe below regulatory limits for all those who are all involved in nuclear storage areas. They ensure that sufficient training in radiation safety rules and protective steps are undertaken by all users.

Radiation Protection Rules (RPR) 2004 is adhered to strictly at all places and time. They issue license to the authorized users of the radioactive materials. These authorized personnel will maintain records containing the procedures and safety rules pertaining to radioactive materials stored. They hold a degree in Science or Post graduate degree in Radiological Physics. A competent authority has to approve his qualifications. They are entrusted with responsibility like chalking out radiation protection program, which should be followed and practiced meticulously.

Safety drill

If any radiation leak is detected or suspected, then it will be recorded for necessary action. He also takes care to see that radiation monitoring gadgets are properly fine tuned and check for its genuineness. Safety drill is conducted to all personnel to see that they manage any emergency. Communication without delay is ensured to avoid calamity. All details of doses of the workers are recorded along with the radioactive materials stored. Once in 4 months the RSO conducts review meeting to see that safety aspects are followed in storage zone. Any incidents like diarrhea, vomiting, suffocation, dizziness and reddish skin are immediately recorded and communicated to higher-ups for action.

As the total dose received by an individual is directly proportional to the time spent close to radioactive source, steps are taken by RSO to reduce that time for all engaged with radioactive materials.

Safeguard Practices

Maximization of distance from the radioactive source, shielding of Alpha radiation by air, water, paper or any material are followed strictly. Beta particles are shielded by water, glass, plastic etc. But it is difficult to escape from X-rays and Gamma rays. So, natural barriers, trenches, protective shelters are helpful to safeguard from it.

Thermo Luminescent Dosimeters, Film badges and direct reading Dosimeters are used to judge the external dose measurement on individuals. Environmental condition is monitored by Radiation Detectors. For men and women, the limit of occupational exposure is same. But if the women are conceived, then it is viewed cautiously and protected.

The Board of Radiation and Isotope Technology located in Mumbai is the authorized unit to import radioactive materials and a senior nuclear scientist possessing much experience will receive it in his name. RSO will frequently check the radioactive storage unit. The Radiation Safety Cell will be contacted by the user for disposal of radioactive materials. It will be sent back to supplier for safe disposal with correct documentation and record formalities. All details will be communicated to AERB and BRIT.

No modification or re-allocation can be done in labs, where radioactive materials are used. Radiation Safety Cell will give approval in writing for any changes in storage. Personnel Monitoring Badges or Electronic Pocket Dosimeters will be worn by Gamma Cells maintenance staff. RSO will be apprised of all works carried out by them. Those who have undergone rigorous training are allowed to operate Gamma cells.

Symbols for Safety

Radiation symbol is fixed on the rooms accommodating the Gamma cells and also on Gamma cell. The phone numbers of Safety Officers are displayed everywhere to face unexpected explosion or damages.

Safety Suits

Radiation levels in various locations are entered in register. The trained staff engaged in operation and maintenance wear full sleeves apron, mask, cap, shoe covers, gloves and plastic safety glasses.

Radiation survey is done periodically by the authorized users and audited by Radiation Safety Cell.

Disposable gloves and remote handling tongs are used for clearing the contamination. The workers are advised to change their hand gloves frequently and dispose them as radioactive waste item with a plastic bag.

Low Range Survey Meter and Liquid Scintillation Counter are used to detect contamination.

Safety Instructions

Centralized Radioactive source storage facility is available to store the disposed radioactive materials.

Special instructions given to users:

1. Only assigned Dosimeter to be worn.
2. Not to tamper Dosimeter
3. Not to use the Dosimeter in washing machine for clothes washer.
4. To wear whole body badge at the chest level.
5. Dosimeter to be returned to the concerned RSO, if he is expected away on leave for a long period.
6. Not to expose Dosimeter purposely to radiation and moisture
7. Not to exchange Dosimeter with other employees.
8. Only trained persons will be allow to have Dosimeter
9. Radiation safety cell will offer whole body badge to be worn at the waist, underneath a lead apron, for pregnant women employees.
10. For evaluation TLD badges will be sent to Defense Lab once in 4 months.
11. Badges are to be returned in a specific time period and no delay is allowed.
12. Lost Dosimeters should be intimated immediately to Radiation Safety Cell.

The Radiation Protection survey is done during and after radioactive material handling to ensure that contamination is eliminated and necessary follow up is done. The record maintained for survey will have the signature of the surveyor, laboratory layout, areas surveyed, conditions of survey instruments, action to be taken and actions already taken for any mishappenings.

All individuals routinely check their clothing during tea break, lunch break and after their day duty. The doors, cup boards, shelves, refrigerators, cell phones, switches, door mat etc are checked to prevent calamities.

Chemical fume hoods and special iodination cabinets are used for protection.

Caution Signs

Bold and clear sign boards are placed to caution one and all from radiological hazards. Each sign has the magenta, purple or black three bladed caution symbols on a yellow back ground with a suitable message like 'Caution Radiation area', 'Caution Radioactive material' etc.

All containers utilized for transporting or storing radioactive materials will have the label 'Caution Radioactive materials'. The type and quantities with date are also seen in all labels.

Empty containers are thoroughly made free from these labels.

If any equipment is age old or poor in quality, we experience air borne radio activity issues. The safety department will ensure that preventive measures are taken imminently.

Safe Transportation

Radiation Safety Cell checks while transportation to see that required quantity permitted by AERB is alone transported for storage.

Packages approved by AERB with radiation symbols are only transported.

The radiation level on the surface of the package is measured by RSO. The quantity of activity will be mentioned on the package. The logbook maintained by RSO will have details of storage, location, date, time of supply, name of the individual carrying the package etc for future reference and action. A copy of the details will be given to the Security Guard section at the gate.

Any error committed in disposal of radioactive waste will lead to severe health problems to outsiders. This will be questioned in the Parliament also.

Before procurement of radioactive material, they plan with vision for correct method for disposal as per rules designed by Radiation Safety Cell.

The waste storage area will be close to work area to avoid spillage problems when transferring waste to containers. Liquid wastes are kept in secondary containment. Each has a label on all sides cautioning radioactive material. Employees are cautioned not to place any radioactive material near the regular dust bins. The identification of containers will be clear and specific.

Without prior permission, different isotopes are not dumped in the same container. No radioactive waste is stored in the lab for a long period. Within a specified time it is disposed off.

The card board boxes used for disposal will be checked before throwing it into trash after disposal works.

Guard at the Gate

The frequent complaints received here is the danger due to spillage of radioactive material or solution. A trained lab worker will be engaged to clear it. Outside agencies are called for major contamination taking place in the premises. The names of persons engaged in the area where spillage occurred will be noted down. Immediate medical attention will be rendered to them after thorough medical checkup. No individual is allowed to go out from the spilled area until they are permitted by safety officials. No outsider will be allowed by the guard at the gate, when any untoward incident has happened inside that area.

All persons not involved in the hazardous area are sent out by the security guard. The room in which the contamination has happened is isolated or locked. A Radiation Safety Cell has been arranged to call them during any calamities. Without their permission no material should be thrown to dustbin or no one should leave without medical checkup.

Alarming Dangers

The anti-nuclear groups never fail to raise their voice about the alarming dangers to society through this nuclear technology.

It's true that nuclear storage in India needs up gradation.

****

Crude Oil and Gas Storage in India

Vital Factor

Storage of Crude oil and gas is a vital factor in any country.

In India much attention is given by experts for this. It is said that Thailand has Crude oil stock for 22 days and China has crude oil stock for 20 days. Oil importing member countries of IEA have commitments to hold stocks equivalent to 90 days of net oil imports.

India has crude oil storage for 19 days. It has 7.3 million tons of crude tank age and 6.8 million tones product tank age capacity. The Public Sector undertakings in oil industry monitor the requirements.

The Petroleum Ministry and Indian oil experts have taken some good steps to establish storage of 5 million metric tons of crude oil in Vishakapattinam, Mangalore and Udupi at a cost of Rs.1650 crores. An investment of Rs.5000 crores would be invested to set up this project within 3 years.

Bikaner is a district in Rajasthan state. This place has been earmarked by ONGC for crude oil storage. The storage will be in full swing next year.

The Engineers India experts have pinpointed a spot for erection of bunkers under the rocks in Udipi which is in Dakshina Karnataka. It's a popular pilgrim centre and also jeweler's work spot. Indian Naval base is also near it with a name Sea-Bird. Though the environmentalist rose with hue and cry, the government was stern in this progress, as this will be the first underground crude bunker in unlined rock cavern, at a depth of 150 ft.

25 to 30% annual consumption of gas is stored in countries like France, Austria etc. But Spain leads them with 35 days reserve.

The Indian gas experts have formed a team and after brainstorming discussion decided to utilize the abandoned gas wells and salt caverns for gas storage.

The other type of gas storage facilities available in India are 1) depleted reservoirs and or gas fields 2) Aquifers 3) Salt caverns.

The first method is widely used in India for its economy and high storage capacity. The second method of storage mentioned alone needs greater supervision. Also it is preferred for gas storage if the water bearing sedimentary rock formation is overlaid with an impermeable cap rock. It also needs base cushion gas and demands care for withdrawal and injection performance.

60,000 mt LPG underground cavern storage is developed in Vishakapattinam at a cost of Rs. 333 crores. A joint venture of HPCL and Total Fina Elf for France are on the job. The storage facilities will be in vogue in the middle of next year.

GAIL India Ltd is on the lookout for a suitable technology for developing gas storage facilities for 15 days at a cost of Rs. 500 crores. The government is keen in developing storage facilities in various locations in India with the technical support of GAIL India Ltd.

****

Food Grain Statistics

- In every year after harvest Rs.55600 crore worth of farm products are spoiled.
- Food grains, alone which are damaged, are to the tune of Rs.16500 crore every year.
- This is 10% of the total agricultural production.
- Dhal varieties to the value of Rs.2000crore get spoiled and thrown as waste. This is also 10% of the total production.
- In the fruit sector 30% are decayed and wasted and worth Rs.15500crore.
- Vegetable also get damaged to the tune of Rs. 14100 crore say the food statisticians.
- As on 30.04.2008 13.4 million tons of wheat has been imported. In 2007 11 million tons of wheat was imported. As on date 22.9 million tons of rice has been imported. Last year 20.9 million tons of rice was imported.
- In India only 29% of available water is saved and used. There is a hot discussion to increase it to 39% o be used by agriculturalists, environmentalists and farm research scholars in India.
- The water we use has only 40% usage capability. Steps are taken to increase it by 50%. With the present water availability only 140million ton food grains are produced. It should be increased by 50million ton more says Mr. Mangala Roy, Director of Indian Agricultural Research Organization. As water quality is going down badly, quantity of water available now will come down by 10%.
- For the past 20 years only 140million ton food production is done in India. This target should be enhanced said the Director in a press meet.
- As the illiterate farmers are unaware of Climatic charges and weather bulletins, the Tamilnadu Government has decided to

install Automatic Weather Monitoring Stations in 224 districts at a cost of Rs.16.90crores. Rain Forecast, Humidity, Suns intensity, Wind direction and Wind force details from these stations will be transmitted to Tamilnadu Agricultural University computer centers. These data will be passed onto farmers once in four days.

- Loss of crops in India due to pests is Rs.1.50 lakhs Crore
- 25% of the total cultivated area of 180 million hectares had been protected from pests.
- The pesticide usage in India is 480 gm/ hectare comparing to other countries like Taiwan, Japan and USA it is far too low. Japan and Taiwan reports 17000 gm/ hectare which is the highest.

The Plant Protection Association of India is situated in Hyderabad where all studies on pesticide usage is done by experts headed by Dr.K.S.R.K Murthy. There 200 companies which deal with crop protection and they have formed an association.

To Enhance Industrial Production in India

Technologies vogue in USA should be honored and welcomed as they are user friendly and can survive for a longer duration with quality, compared to Russian technologies.

To Chalk Out Plans

Entire world knows that industrial production is weak in India.

Even a new born baby will tell that our GDP will never grow in this condition.

The government has to think meticulously and chalk out plans to solve this.

Support from banks to the industrial sector is vital. Several economic experts and media covering financial aspects argued with Reserve Bank to reduce the interest rate for loans. But the top authorities in Reserve Bank were adamant in this regard. Later on they decided to reduce the REPO rate by 0.25% from 8% to 7.75%. So, the reserve funds in Banks were also reduced from 4.25 % to 4 %. By this step the interest rates charged to the small scale industries came down. The common man was also benefitted as housing loan, car loan, personal loan, consumer loans etc came down. This in turn made them to acquire homes, cars, house-hold articles and enabled all the industries involved in these sectors to grow.

As CRR reserve fund was reduced, the banks have Rs 18000 crores of surplus funds and by which they can liberally grant loans to the Indian citizens and entrepreneurs. For the reserve fund possessed by banks, no interest is payable to the Reserve Bank by them. So, the banks earn a lot by giving this fund as loans and the public also enjoy the lower interest benefits.

This trend should continue for industrial production in India. This step should have been taken in 2012 itself. There are two main reasons for it. Reserve Bank usually aims to lower inflation and reduce the rise in price of commodities. Second aim is to give unperturbed loan facilities to industries for economic growth.

With these two aims the reserve bank tries to control inflation and price rise. They hinted to reduce the interest rates but failed to implement it due to absence for alertness and distant vision.

The GDP has fallen down by 0.9% continuously for the past 3 months, which was never witnessed for the past 3 years. It touched 7.2% in December 2012. Reserve Bank expected the inflation by 6.8% in March 2013. This figure was lower than the predicted value by it. But they anticipated that GDP growth will be 5.8% in March 2013. Later on they announced that it will touch only 5.5%. Analyzing this sad situation it decided to reduce the interest by 0.25% to improve industrial production in India.

In 2013, the industrial production had fallen down by 1.1% and export turnover had also fallen down badly.

After a long sleep, the financial experts have decided to set right the turmoil in financial sector. Deficit danger is swallowing India and hence they focused on subsidies where wastages are unbearable. The economic experts planned to give it in cash to the public. To increase revenue, only way is to rise the GDP. Introducing new taxes to meet this demand is not favorable as election is nearby in 2014. People will throw out for their sluggishness and heavy tax burdens.

Due to some economic reforms and changes, the share market has risen to a colorful status, which has attracted foreign investors. In this condition, reserve Bank has taken a last effort by reducing interest rates to screw up the progress. But this action will not support the economic growth and industrial growth in the long run.

The government plays a vital role to encourage entrepreneurs, reduce inflation and boost the GDP. For this we need new investments in infrastructure, clean environment, trouble free and maintenance free imported equipments. A distant vision of the economic magnets is essential to build the image of industrial growth in India. Any emergency action after a long idleness will not do well. Appropriate action at the right time after a good forecast is needed in India. A committee has been formed for the investment sector and plans. All their efforts have to be implemented with dedication and speed. Then only the foreign investments will be lured.

The land acquisition is the major problem in India. The land owners never come forward for any infrastructure development, as the price fixed by the government for their lands will be too low and they have to run after them for years together to get the compensation. Judicial support for the common man is insufficient in India. Small scale industries are not affordable to claim their rights through High Courts and Supreme Court. Hence this affects the industrial growth. The law favors the government and their price fixation for lands and hence suitable amendments have to be introduced to please the land owners, who offer their lands buildings and livelihood for the sake of infrastructure developments.

Market value of the acquired lands is usually far above the value pinpointed by the government. This large gap should be narrowed and reasonable bargaining will alone clear the blocked infrastructure projects essential for industrial growth. The project report submitted by the officials to the planning committee should have all the relevant facts and documents. Clearance from Environmental department, Forest department and Pollution Control Board are usually delayed. The public complain that false clearance reports are prepared without their knowledge and only when major works are commenced they are aware of the few facts of the project. Kudankulam is one important project, where people around it have opposed violently and were ignorant of many technical dangers behind it. Still their agitation continues. Such draw backs are to be eliminated.

Technologies vogue in USA should be honored and welcomed as they are user friendly and can survive for a longer duration with quality, compared to Russian technologies.

Whenever interest rates for loans are reduced, then the rate of interest for saving bank accounts and fixed deposit will go down. This will badly affect the citizens, who depend mainly on bank interest for their daily bread. In the past, when interest for loans were reduced, the rates for fixed deposits were not slashed, because it will affect the common man in the street, who are the buyers of many domestic goods manufactured by small scale industries. So, the reactions of bank towards reduction of fixed deposit will also affect the industrial growth in India.

Banks aim that deposits will raise by 15%, but it is dubious as the people have started investing is gold. So, the banks should never dream of reducing the fixed deposit interest even if the loan interests to the industrialists are reduced.

There is no association or strong chamber for the depositors to fight against the banks. Hence they are at their mercy always. Long-term deposits should be made more attractive so that common man will prefer it, which in turn will not affect them when Reserve Bank orders to reduce the rate of interest. These citizens are back-bones of industrial growth and hence utmost care is to be taken for them.

Food Security Bill

This bill was introduced by Sonia Gandhi with a good and generous heart. Nobody should starve without food is her noble dream and aim.

To erase poverty and hunger, the ruling party wished to introduce this Food Security Bill. The opposition parties ordered for some alterations. But the ruling party experts, who have better vision and knowledge, ignored it. As per the bill, 75% of the Indian population living in villages and 50% in cities will be benefitted. On an average, 67% of the total population will reap benefits, say the rulers.

The economists pronounce that this 67% will vary from State to State. But the members of Central Planning Committee have already submitted the percentage of beneficiaries in each State, to the Food ministry.

Some leaders argue that in 13States out of 21 States, the percentage of population to get this benefit will be less that 67%. Particularly in Tamilnadu, 62.55% of the populations are in villages and 37.79% are in cities. So, by adding both, the percentage of beneficiaries will be only 50.55%, as said by the rulers.

For example in the present condition, 90% of the population in Tamilnadu enjoys the food supply scheme adopted by the State government. So, the new bill which covers 67% will be lower than the present status. The calculation given by the Food Security bill is that 50.55% of the population will be benefitted in this Tamilnadu State. This will doom the opportunities of the remaining citizens. In Tamilnadu 49% live in cities. But as per the bill only 37.79% will get the benefit and the remaining will be left out totally, say the BJP.

The Central government should not decide the number of persons to be benefitted in each State, as it is against the coalition style of rule.

Opposition members say that as per the bill submitted to Parliament, 35 kilos of rice will be given to each family. But after an emergency modification, it was made as 5 kilos/individual. Hence for a family with 5 members, the government will offer 25 kilos and for a family with 3 members it will not offer 20 kilos of rice and wheat, as done now in Kerala.

The new order for food supply will definitely reduce the quantity already supplied by Tamilnadu government. At present 296000 tons food grains are allocated to Tamilnadu by the Central government. But as per the new bill, this State will lose 1 lakh tons of food supply. In order to continue the present supply, the State government has to procure food grains from open market at high price, which will be a big loss to treasury, say the opposition members. A burden of Rs.3000 crore will fall on the head of the Tamilnadu ruler.

This is only an example. Similar situation will be witnessed in other States too, say the BJP leaders. Obviously they oppose it firmly.

The economic experts feel that the food supply arrangements now made by the Tamilnadu State ruler is not a wise move, as the quantity released at free of cost is too high and done with a vote bank policy. Hence the new food policy prescribed by the Central government will be safe and sound for a longer duration.

The Congress leaders sincerely aim that Indian citizens, who are gripped by malnutrition should be fed well and there should be security in their daily food needs. That's why this bill was introduced by Sonia Gandhi with a good and generous heart. Nobody should starve without food is her noble aim. Cry for daily bread should not be heard in India, is her holy dream.

Opposition, who always pounce to shatter good moves, should understand that such policies are introduced for the welfare of the nation and not for escalating the status of Congress or any particular individual. A broad outlook lacks in opposition party. They do not favor the Congress leaders to be in the good books of the downtrodden Indians, as they seek their votes in the ensuing election.

If Food Security Bill brings a sea of change in family daily needs, then the opposition can never dream of capturing majority of the votes. So, to disturb this trend, they create hue and cry against this bill totally. They don't want to lose the goodwill of the villagers as food security bill will wipe the fears and tears of many millions. Some corrections are always welcomed by the ruling party. Some political members feel that many will be deprived of getting food supply under this scheme, which will be considered meticulously by the food experts in Delhi.

The opposition parties' demands:

1. Apart from those who pay tax, others should also be covered by this Food Security Bill.
2. This bill focus only on rice, wheat etc., but it should covers sugar, dhal, cooking oil etc also.
3. Each individual should be offered 7 kilo or 35 kilos of food grains should be given for a family.
4. As per the price fixed by the bill, rice will be given at Rs.3/kilo. But it should be given at Rs.2/kilo.
5. It is stated in the bill that the price of food grains will be in force for 3 years and after that it will be revised as per the price fluctuation. This will lead to cut in subsidy given for food supply and the base price of the food grains. So, this condition should be erased.
6. Central government will have the full authority to decide about the sharing of expenses, which is objectionable. The State government should be consulted beforehand and the bill should function with their consultation and approval only.
7. This bill aims to eliminate food supply through community food supply plans, which will affect the backward community citizens. So, the government should shoulder the expenses towards it.
8. Under no condition, the present food supply to each State should not be cut or reduced.
9. Offering money using Adhaar card should be banned.

The above mentioned demands are not reasonable.

Asking for the rulers to cover sugar, dhal, cooking oil etc is beyond the limits but even then the rulers are always prepared to widen the food supply at the right time. The demand for 7 kilos/ individual is also not acceptable. The government has already reduced the price as Rs 3/kilo instead of Rs 5 and in this condition to ask for Rs2/kilo is also not a reasonable demand.

Moreover the Centre is always prepared for any open discussion with all States and prefers transparency in all issues. The required consultations with State Chiefs will be done at all stages. The government has no intention to interfere matters related to religion and they mainly aim to eliminate the malpractices done in the name of communal feelings. Due to wide circulation of bogus ration cards, this Bill stressed the need of AADHAR card as they are fool proof identification for the Indian citizens. The record of eye ball is an added advantage in this card system.

Opposition members always aim to get the support of people, who have thrown them down in yester years due to utter failure in their ruling capabilities. People know who is worthy to rule India and who can sustain for 5 years in spite of many oppositions, brick bats and false cases. The Centre is strong and knowledgeable and at the same time flexible in this coalition rule. That's why they could hold on for 5 years. The President of the Congress party has matured approach in all Bills introduced in the Parliament and never let down the common man in the street.

The aim of Food Security Bill is also to fulfill that honorable move.

****